Ghost Stories of Sutton Coldfield

Ghost Stories of Sutton Coldfield

Patrick B. Hayes

BREWIN
BOOKS

First published in July 2000 by
Brewin Books, Studley, Warwickshire.

© Patrick B. Hayes 2000
All rights reserved.

ISBN 1 85858 168 0

Photography by Michael Madden.
Illustrations by Andrew Spencer.

British Library Cataloguing in Publication

A catalogue record for this book is available
from the British Library

Typeset in Palatino and
made and printed in Great Britain by
SupaPrint (Redditch) Ltd.,
Redditch, Worcestershire.
Website: www.supaprint.com
E-mail: admin@supaprint.com

Acknowledgements

Dedicated to my dear friend, Carmen, with love.

I would like to thank the following with all their help in making this book possible.

Patricia Sinsheimer, Marian Baxter, Robert Pritchard, Julia Bowden, David Owen OBE, Grace Jenkins, Jean Jones, Caroline Parkes, Helen, Deckland Jedd, Brian Walwork, Margaret Bennett, Angela Evans, Mrs Higgs, Jane Haywood, John Bailey, Margaret Lampitt, Mr Pickering, Mr Mc Kian, Martin Bissell, Karl Bramwell, Christine Lambert, Wendy Barnes, Clare Hayes, Gwyn Thomas, Steve Andrews, Sue Fenoughty - Sue, Mavis, Jill, Marian & Sue at the Hungry Horse Tea Rooms..

The road out of Birmingham is not the best.

C.P.Moritz when journeying to Sutton Coldfield from Birmingham.

"Journeys of a German in England in 1782."

Introduction

Most people have heard of Sutton Coldfield. Most of them have been known to pronounce it, COALFIELD, as they conjure up images of grinning white teeth through coal-covered faces, cranking pit head machinery and hills of shiny black coal. However, many people are bemused on discovering that the name is Coldfield. Apparently it is possible to draw a straight line from the Urals in Russia, through central Europe, across the North sea, over the Norfolk broads and finally to Sutton Coldfield. The straight line will not come across any mountain range or high terrain until Sutton and that is why it is known as Sutton Coldfield! It probably makes sense, as nearby West Bromwich has a football team whose ground is the highest above sea level. A very useful fact if entering a pub quiz! Historians have argued over the derivative of the town's name, one of the ideas being it is derived from when Sutton was in Mercia. It means quite simply that it is the town south of Tamworth and it lies on the side of a hill, possibly where charcoal is burnt.

Although now officially in Birmingham, Sutton was known, and still is, as The Royal Town of Sutton Coldfield. As a child I remember the old wooden post bearing the name and coat of arms which stood at the town's boundary at the Yenton where the Corporation buses of the city would stop. However, the larger, more attractive Midland Red, with softer seats, would carry on to such unknown and far away places as Roughley or Tamworth. Far away places indeed in the mind of a child, as was the vastness of Sutton Park.

Today with the advancement of car ownership it is common to drive to Weston or Wales for the day but before the abundance of cars a wonderful day of virtual rustic delight could be spent in the park. I remember one particular Sunday after spending a long, enjoyable summer's day in the park walking back to Gravelly Hill along the railway line. Although highly illegal, my friends and I felt safe, as local trains didn't run on a Sunday. We kicked along the tracks as the evening sun fell, chatting about the day's adventures. It was like a scene in the famous film, "Stand By Me."

Now, Sutton conjures up images of Henry the Eighth hunting in the forest which is now the park, the stern looking figure of Bishop Vesey and what was the magnificent Great Northern Railway Hotel that gives such a commanding view of the town and park. Take away the modern Gracechurch shopping centre, the large municipal buildings and the roads choked with cars and the journey into the past can begin. As with every village in England, there were those that lived and worked before us. Like people today they had hopes, fears, worried about the weather, gossiped about neighbours and plodded or ploughed through the cycle of rural life.

Looking at maps, pictures and especially old photographs gives us a treasured and privileged look into the world of the past. I always find it fascinating that as we are now so they were then but like leaves , in an autumn breeze they have silently fallen and blown away forever. So it would seem. But maybe there are still echoes and shadows from that world, the world of the past that still lingers on, that still stay with us.

Contents

The Roman Centurion.

Perhaps the oldest feature of Sutton is the Roman road, ICKNIELD STREET that passes through the park. This ancient walk stretched from Bourton-on-the Water to Wall, just outside Lichfield. It was also the main road to Watling Street and certainly would have Legionaries marching along it.

When walking along the centuries old Ickneild Street it is possible to turn back the years as it is a place of great solitude. However, it is best to avoid a glance towards Hill Village where there is a reminder of the twenty- first century. The tall, sleek television mast, which can be seen for miles and from the surrounding three counties, along with the hum of the distant traffic is of this age. If such intrusions can be forgotten the pages of the past can be turned back and the journey into a different time can be made.

It is here that our first story begins. Nowadays, the old Roman road looks more like a path through a wood than a feat of Roman/Britannic civil engineering. Historians have also noted that more than a few Roman soldiers lost their lives whilst constructing the roads and may be their memories are still there in the park.

According to local legend it is said that the figures of legionaries can be seen marching down Ickneild Street. At other times, their disembodied voices shouting orders can be heard. Their voices are carried on the wind that sweeps across the open parkland.

Roman Soldier

Henry V111 and the rattling door!

There are other stories of strange goings on related to Sutton Park. Imagine if you can, living in a delightful, almost idyllic, cottage by one of the many splendid lakes in the park. The gamekeeper's cottage is now a café and the year is 1976. The Tearooms are now closed, the floors swept, the kitchen cleaned the lights switched off, all ready for another day. The lady of the café is going to bed. Her husband plays in a Big Band and will not be home for some time.

The lady, Mrs Sinsheimer, tired from the day's work goes to bed. She has a restless night and soon wakes. She hears a noise coming from the window. She gingerly clambers out of her bed and makes to where the noise is coming from. Maybe it was just the wind sweeping across the lake or the breeze through the branches in the woods.

With little or no light she walks to the window. For a moment she thinks that she is still dreaming. She closes her eyes and opens them quickly. But no, she is not dreaming and there in the window is a face. It is a familiar face. Nearly everyone would recognise it, as it is the face of Henry the Eighth. She is not scared but the dog growls and goes under the bed. She has described her experience as being, "Startled"

In Henry's day, Sutton Park was known as Sutton Chase and locals will readily tell of the days when King Henry would leave the noise and stench of Tudor London for the refreshing spaces of the Chase! Lodged at the Driffold, the horses would canter up Manor Hill and then break into a furious gallop down into the chase. The huntsmen, headed by Henry would eagerly look forward to the day's hunt. The poor, unsuspecting creature would be hunted till he could run no further. The spoils of war would then be carried ceremoniously back into the Royal Town where a feast awaited.

Another night at the old gamekeeper's cottage the lady along with her husband heard noises coming from outside of the cottage. The clock had struck midnight and there was a definite noise coming from outside. "An unholy row" could be heard coming from where the stables used to be. They both went to investigate but fear prevented them from going further than the kitchen door. The sound, like the face in the window was easily recognisable. The heavy sound that was beating on the ground was the sound of horse's hooves! As they stood at the kitchen door they could hear the sound of horses galloping across the park, or should that be the Chase? They also could hear the sound of running water and logs tumbling down a stream. The noise was clearly audible and there was no mistake as to what it was.

Then they heard footsteps coming up the path towards the café. They were so scared that they put the furniture against the door. They waited. They looked at the door and noticed the handle turn! They phoned the police and after about three hours the police turned up to find everything quiet and just as it was before. It was pitch black and the police said that the gates had been locked when they arrived.

Bracebridge Cottage where noises of a hunt were heard.

4

Ghostly Hooves.

Mr and Mrs Sinsheimer are not the only ones to experience ghostly galloping. In the 1980's, two women, Mother and Daughter, along with their two dogs were taking a brisk stroll through the park. It was a summer's afternoon and they had just walked past the Jamboree stone that lies near the open heath land. On they walked, chatting, letting the dogs enjoy the open spaces of the heath, when suddenly they heard the sound of a horse cantering behind them. Nothing unusual in that, as many riders are seen in the park. They took no notice at first but their complacence soon turned to anxiety as the cantering steps got faster and faster, closer and closer. "Look out!" the mother cried, as she thought the horse was about to run through them. The two women jumped out of the way of the galloping steed. They looked up expecting to see the beast rush by. However, much to their amazement, they were staring into fresh air!

They looked around; the dogs had been oblivious to it all as they scampered about in the bushes in their bid for new adventures. The women, slightly shaken, walked on. This incident took place near the Jamboree Stone yet Mr and Mrs Sinsheimer's experience took place at Bracebridge Pool, which is on the other side of the park!

Out of all the tales of Sutton, this gentle reader may be the most fascinating. As with nearly all experiences with the paranormal it was brief but unforgettable.

The place where the two ladies experienced the ghostly galloping lies in a deserted, if not bleak, part of the park. It is covered in prickly gorse now, but years ago, lying so open, it probably was similar to Shakespeare's, "Blasted heath,"

On first inspection it would seem strange that anyone would come this way where the ladies said they heard the sound. However, on closer inspection the gorse bushes hang over a narrow but well- worn path. It is too small to be a bridle path but large enough for walkers and the occasional rider too.

The path meanders somewhat and leads to a copse of trees that stand on a hill. A copse on a blasted heath seems strange at first, even out of place. It then makes sense. When standing inside the copse it is possible to make out the traces of buildings. For on that spot lay Rowton Cottage, a farmhouse long since gone. The view from the cottage looks down onto Rowton's Well, disused and derelict. In the distance the old Roman road, Chester Road, can be made out. However, the well was once a hive of activity. People from outside the area had heard of the well's medicinal properties. Apparently the salts in the water, rather like spa water, could even cure chronic diseases and worked particularly with children and slim people!

Those that lived in Rowton Cottage were not the only ones who once lived in sight of Rowton's Well. Centuries before, Centurions and their soldiers camped near the site. Which brings us to the question. Who was the rider of the horse that the ladies heard that afternoon? Was it a member of the Rowton Household galloping home through the wind and the rain looking forward to an open fire and dry clothes? Some one galloping towards the well in search of a desperate remedy? Or was it a Roman soldier bringing news of impending attack or news from home and warmer climes?

It is also a well known fact that Lord Donegal from Swifen Hall came to the park twice a year to hunt. Horses and riders would come through what was known as the Royal Oak Gate, near the Chester Road and gallop off in chase of the deer. The Lord's ride went as far as the Jamboree Stone, which is very near where the two ladies had their ghostly experience. So maybe, it was Lord Donegal or one of his huntsmen that day?

It is often thought that experiences like the ghostly thundering of hooves are an echo of the past, similar in that remarkable scene in Powell and Pressburger's CANTERBURY TALE. During the Second World War an American soldier stationed in Kent out walking one summer's day puts his ear to the ground and for a few moments he can hear voices from a different time. Although an echo at first, the sound slowly grows louder and what the young GI can hear are the voices and noises of Chaucer's characters as they canter slowly towards Canterbury.

Did our two ladies have a similar experience, except this time it was not fiction? An anonymous local historian from the eighteenth century, who signed himself, "An impartial hand," informs his readers that wild horses used to roam around what is now the park. Maybe this is what the mother and daughter witnessed that afternoon?

However, it is not only a King and his Horses that seem to visit the park but ordinary couples from another time, another place.

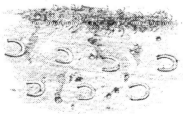

Windswept heath near Rowten's Well where
Ghostly Hooves were heard.

The Courting Couple and the Stagecoach.

A local lady was walking her dog, one day, by Boldmere gate, when she noticed a young man and woman in the distance standing by the woods. At first she thought nothing of it and walked on. It was only after coming slightly closer to them that she realised that their dress was of the early nineteenth century. She walked on but curiosity got the better of her and she soon returned. Perhaps a film or television programme was being made? But when she returned the couple were no longer there. However, she distinctly remembers the couple. They were young and patiently waiting. For a coach perhaps? She also remembers the young man gently adjusting the lady's cloak that had fallen slightly from her slim shoulders. He gently placed it back in position protecting his lady from the inclement weather, so it seems. So cogent was the experience that she wrote the incident down and sent it to a magazine called "Country Living" in January 1996. The Editor of the magazine was so impressed by the encounter that she published it for her readers to share.

A more recent tale that has occurred is from a local man called Martin. Martin is currently a postman and one early morning in January he was driving to work. It was about 4.30. And he was driving near the park by Wyndley Swimming Baths, which backs onto the park. He was driving along on an empty road when he suddenly braked as something ran out in front of him. The car came to a sudden halt, the engine still purring in the early wintry morning. Martin sat there for a moment, staring in disbelief. It wasn't a cat that had ran across the road or even a local heading for the morning newspaper but clearly and without a shadow of a doubt, a carriage and horses!

Martin looked around the empty Wyndley Lane to see it as deserted as a desert. However, he testified that he saw a "Black Coach" with a man driving the carriage. He was wearing, "An old fashioned hat" and that there were, "At least two horses."

Was this the coach that was going to collect our romantic couple in the park seen by a lady near Boldmere Gate? Wyndley Lane is an ancient lane that was used by the cattle drovers taking. It was also the only road that led into the park until the 1800's'

It is also interesting to note that the two English teachers that experienced the well-known sightings at Versailles in France also experienced seeing a coach and horses going at great speed through the palace grounds. Maybe Sutton is not to be overshadowed by the events in France!

Before we leave the park it is well worth noting another strange and inexplicable experience. Our friends at Bracebridge had been having a family gathering. After the night's joviality their guests departed. A convoy of cars headed out of the darkness of the park towards the park gate. As they drove past the railway line all of the cars' headlights dimmed. The electric on all the cars seemed to lose power for several seconds only to regain full power as they left the side of the railway line. This seems to be more in keeping with those that experience UFO phenomena than images and sounds from the past!

Whatever, the park, once the Royal Chase, seems to hold secrets that are, to this day, unexplained!

The Ghost of the Cavalier in the Three Tuns Hotel.

The loud music booms, which almost make the room, shake and shudder. Young people, mainly students from the local F.E. College, tap their feet to the rhythm of the disco beat. Chats about cars, Aston Villa, who's dating who, crackle around the noisy, dimly lit room.

However, unknown to most of the young people distracted in their diversions this was once home to a different type of reveller. It was a time when wooden wheeled coaches would rattle over the cobblestones and into the courtyard of the Three Tuns Hotel. Many a night the Three Tuns gave shelter from the storm.

As the young people dance and drink the night away they are unaware that in the cellars under them there is another young man, from another place, another time. Yet this young man has no interest in fast cars or football teams because he belongs to the seventeenth century, when the English Civil War raged across the English countryside.

The story is told of the sad Cavalier who haunts the dark, dusty cellars under The Tuns Hotel. It is here, so it is said, that the cellars are part of a net work of tunnels that spread under the old houses of the High Street. Furthermore, there is a tunnel, now bricked up, that leads from the medieval church of Holy Trinity to the sixteenth century coaching house. In the early Eighties, the local newspaper, "The Sutton News," along with a local radio station, embarked upon a two-night vigil in the cellars in the hope of meeting the young man. One autumn night as it approached Hallowe'en, the pub landlord, Daryl, along with a young, female intrepid reporter, called Sue, began to knock a hole in the three centuries old wall. Behind the wall, they were hoping to find the ancient tunnel that led from the hotel to the church. They were both nervous, nervous over what gruesome discovery would be found. Only a few years before Declan, the young barman, had stepped into the cellars where he heard the distinct noise of metal clashing upon metal. "Like chain mail being dragged across the floor," was Declan's description. But he also heard a voice. The voice, that came from the deep darkness of the dank cellars was clear, audible and it said, "Who goes there?" in quite a military tone. Declan has sworn there was no one else in the cellar and was more than confident in stating that he was not the victim of a practical joke.

Around the same time a young barmaid also went down into the dark cellars. It was time for the pub to close and as she was locking up she heard a noise down the cellars. She thought at first it must be a colleague and, fearful that he might be locked in for the night went down. She soon returned, ashen faced and silent. She did not say a word but left that night and to this day she has never returned.

It was the plethora of stories that led to both the newspaper and radio station taking the steps of setting up a vigil. Maybe behind the wall would lie the bones of the young Cavalier, bones, that, if found, Daryl insisted, would be later buried in consecrated ground allowing, the young man to find peace instead of restlessly wandering the cellars of the pub.

Imaginations ran wild, as the bricks of the new wall that sealed the entrance to the sixteenth century tunnels were removed. There had been rumours for years in the town that a monk's retreat existed in the maze of tunnels that ran under the High Street. When the bricks were removed a three-foot gap was discovered which led to an ancient looking wall which had a seven-inch hole in the bottom.

Like a disappointing climax to what should have been an exciting film, nothing was found. Despite digging and removing bricks over the next few days the labours of Daryl and Sue came to naught. However, what still remained were the stories of the Cavalier that would not go away.

Those that have seen this young man, say he is both handsome and dashing. One of the landlords of the pub, Jimmy Trigg, actually did see the young, dashing cavalier one morning in the cellars. He was with his dog, Jaffa. Jimmy was going about his daily routine when he felt a tap on his shoulder. He turned around and there before him, as clear as anything, was a fine, good looking, young lad who said, "Excuse me." When Jimmy looked at the smiling face of the young Cavalier he disappeared in front of his eyes. Jaffa, the dog turned tail and fled up the cellar steps into the apparent safety of the pub and Jaffa could never be persuaded to go back into the cellars again. The apparition was described as wearing, "A beautiful blue velvet suit with a ruffle at his neck and black patent shoes with large buckles. He had long black hair and a young face."

Although Jimmy felt shocked at the time he did not think that the figure was frightening and he later said, "I never feel alone in this building."

As well as being seen in the cellar the Cavalier has also been heard in other rooms in the pub. When the assistant manager told this boss that the local papers and radio were coming to investigate, a large glass mirror that sat on the dresser in the Landlord's bedroom shattered into a thousand tiny pieces. Also, the young Cavalier has a "Sense of humour" according to Daryl. He wanders all over the building. One day the dog was locked in an unused room. The room has a Yale lock and cannot be closed from the outside without a key. However, Darryl returned to find the door wide open and the poor dog all of a shiver. The dog had never been in that room before and refused to go back in there again. Was the young man playing tricks on his twentieth-century landlord or did he simply wish to release the dog from a locked room?

So what do we know of our phantom friend at the Tuns? He is dressed as a cavalier and fought for the doomed forces of the king. But why should this dashing young man, hide amongst the barrels and pumps of the pub?

One theory is that, as the Royalist forces began to lose the fight and the Parliamentarians gained the upper hand, he hid, perhaps wounded, from Cromwell's efficient and ruthless army. The forces of Parliament had attacked Aston Hall in the next parish and Lichfield to the north had been under siege. Erdington born, Hervey Bagot, Governor of Lichfield, had been killed endeavouring to keep Cromwell's men at bay. Two of the town's important figures lent their support to Cromwell and the Parliamentarian forces. It is said that Oliver Cromwell himself stayed at the Tuns.

The Pudsey family, who lived at Langly Hall, supported Cromwell and the Rector of Sutton, Anthony Burgess is described as being, "A Puritan divine of considerable repute." (MIDGLEY)

Although there was military activity at nearby Aston Hall, where King Charles stayed, the war did not directly effect Sutton. Prince Rupert, King Charles's nephew, did pass through the town after winning a battle at Birmingham's Camp Hill. The dashing, fearless Cavalier wanted to punish Birmingham for its support of Cromwell and, after looting and burning Birmingham he headed north towards Lichfield. The Prince passed peacefully through Sutton, which makes it more of a mystery why the ghost of a young cavalier is seemingly "trapped" in the "Three Tuns."

Is it possible that our young friend, a local man and supporter of the Royalist cause, fell foul of sympathisers of Cromwell after Prince Rupert had passed through the town?

If this was so it could be said that he simply was in the wrong place at the wrong time. According to stories that have been handed down over the years he was put in the stocks of the town where he was stoned by angry townsfolk and, after being severely wounded, was brought to the Three Tuns where he died on account of injuries suffered in the stoning. But why should a young man be pilloried in such a way? Were the townspeople of the "Royal " Town siding with Cromwell and simply seeing the young lad as the enemy? Or was it soldiers from the soon to be, Lord Protector that dragged him through the town displaying him as a trophy of war. The battered and bruised body in his brightly coloured attire would be a salutary reminder to anyone who wanted to fight or side with the Royalist cause. If they donned the colours of the King and took to the flag, they also would soon discover Parliamentarian justice.

Another theory is that the young man is Scottish, as he was a member of the Duke of Hamilton's army! In 1648 Cromwell defeated Hamilton's army at Preston, Lancashire. Those who survived were taken prisoner and taken on the slow, arduous journey south to London, where they would be transported to the Colonies.

The local people were appalled when they saw the dejected prisoners pass through the town. They were virtually dying from starvation as they only had the scraps off the land to eat. Maybe our young man in the Three Tuns was one of those unfortunate beings and, too weak to continue his journey, because of hunger and wounds, was abandoned to die on the floor of a Warwickshire Hostelry, miles from his native Scotland?

Whatever happened that fateful day in the Royal Town no one will know. However, if the first account is true and a young cavalier was put in the stocks his disgrace and humiliation were not enough as he suffered fatal blows, blows that led to his death on the cold cellar floor of the coaching house. Worse was to follow, according to one local source. As if not dying without dignity was not enough, the poor boy was denied a Christian burial as his body was taken to one of the tunnels where it was bricked up.

It is quite distressing to think that such a young man lay bleeding, dying in the dank cellar, his cause lost, with no hand to hold, with no Angel at his side. Maybe he died there and even after all these years he is too scared, frightened, to venture out and leave the apparent safety of The Three Tuns.

Three Tuns Hotel where a young cavalier haunts cellars.

The young cavalier

Things that go bump in the night at New Hall Mill.

There is a mill in New Hall in Sutton Coldfield. It lies between Bishop Walsh Catholic School and the Four Star Hotel, New Hall, where such famous people as Diana Ross and Pavaroti stay when performing in Birmingham. It can be found just off the Wylde Green Road as the road curves upward towards the Birmingham Road that leads into Sutton Town centre. It was not so long ago that Wylde Green Road was a country lane. The road narrowed when it came to the small stone bridge that stood over the river Ebrook. It was so narrow that trees formed an archway over the lane. Shadows of the trees would cast themselves on the lane that eventually led to the haunted mill!

The story goes that one night a young woman who lived in the house went to the Still Room during the night for a glass of milk. She stepped onto one of the old, stone flagstones and, as she did, she found herself unable to move, as if she was glued to the spot! After a few moments her temporary prison came to an end. Terrified, she ran back to bed without her glass of milk.

One chilly night she was sitting before the open coal fire with her father and stepmother. It was a peaceful evening; the only sound that could be heard was the gentle rustle coming from the pages of the newspaper being turned as her father read silently by the fire. The two ladies of the house saw, much to their amazement, the large heavy cast iron oven door slowly, silently but surely open and, as slowly as it opened, it closed again. The woman went to tell her father but her step mother stopped her and signalled to her not to say a word, as she was sure he would only ridicule them.

It seems there has been a ghost at the mill for some time now. There was an account of the ghost given in 1890 and it is thought that it may have been a woman who worked in the kitchen at the time.

A man called Ben Davis had experiences of the mill's ghost when he lived at the mill. As a child, he recalled the many times he and his father heard a sharp knocking at the door. When the door was opened there was no one there! Ben's sister, Mary, says she lost count of how many times they went to answer the door only to discover an empty porch.

Ben also remembers another account. One evening, when he was about twelve years old, he went out with his father, leaving his mother alone in the house. Ben came home that day slightly earlier than his father and found his mother in a most agitated and confused state. She told Ben that after they had left for the day she had decided to sit downstairs and take a well-earned rest. She was only sitting for a few moments when she heard noises. The noises were coming not from outside the mill but directly above the room she was sitting in. At first she was not sure what the noise was but then, after a few moments, when her initial fear had passed, she recognised the scraping and banging as the furniture being moved around the bedroom!

Ben's mother asked him to investigate. He nervously lit a candle and, with a trembling hand, he slowly began to climb the wooden steps. The stairs were steep and hollow sounding. Gingerly, Ben walked up the stairs. The light flickered, casting shadows against the wall. As he thought what might confront him in the bedroom, his heart beat faster, his palms became sweaty and the hairs on the back of his neck began to stand up like bristles.

He slowly turned the handle of the bedroom door and at a push, the door flew open. He held the candle up to give him light as the room was in virtual darkness. He peered into the gloom, the candle-light slowly seeping light into the blackness. He took a sigh of relief. The room was completely empty, and moments later, much to his mother's disbelief, the bedroom furniture had not been moved an inch. Is this the case of a mischievous spirit that enjoys frightening people or was it a flashback in time? Had Ben's mother had unwittingly heard another person from another time dutifully going about their daily chores? If so there was nothing spooky or sinister but simply the case of some ghostly housework being done!

When Ben was a child and his father was going through his normal chores at the mill they saw a stranger walking down the lane towards them. He was an elderly gentleman and he told them the reason of his visit. Many years ago he had lived at the mill and he too had experienced strange happenings!

He later talked to Ben's mother and he asked her if she had ever heard the cast iron oven doors open and close on their own. She told the elderly gentleman that she too had experienced the comings and goings of the mill's ghost. It seems that the elderly gentleman and Ben's family was able to confirm that the presence in the house confined his or her activities to the house.

However, a gentleman called Harold Fisher who now lives in Merseyside had a different tale to tell! He recalled the time when his mother would often tell him of the ghostly goings on at the mill when she lived there as a young girl. Much to Harold's astonishment, she would tell of the times, when during the early hours of the morning, heavy noises could be heard coming from under the mill. When asked what the noises sounded like, she answered, "Like horses clumping around." She also told the tale of how her father, Edward Caldicott, when hearing the noises, would venture outside.

With lantern in hand and accompanied by a fellow workman, Edward would search and look everywhere for the source of the noise, but to no avail! The mystery of the mill continues!

New Hall Mill site of strange noises and goings on!

Bedroom at mill where furniture was heard moving about.

The Warlock of New Hall and other stories.

One of the oldest inhabited houses in the parish of Sutton Coldfield is New Hall. It is one of the most picturesque, described as "The moated stone mansion" by one local historian.

In the days when most people saw the world on a black and white t.v screen, Marilyn Monroe was the star of the day, and it wasn't unusual for Bolton Wanderers to win the F.A.Cup, several children like the characters in Enid Blyton's, The Famous Five went on amazing adventures.

The children lived with their parents, Mr and Mrs Owen, in a rambling, Victorian house called The Highway, virtually secluded from view and nestling comfortably by eighteenth century pillars that once harnessed iron gates. If this was not exciting enough, down the drive lay further delights. Down, down the drive they would go and soon what would seem like a fairy castle would come into view. Flags fluttered from a castle tower, a moat lay still around the mansion and the sun glinted on the numerous windows that lined the broad brickwork. It was New Hall, looking majestic in the morning sun. In the tower, there was a hidden room where no one had been, a room without doors or steps. What secrets lay in the room raced around in the children's imagination? One of the young boys tried to find out by scaling the old ivy walls of the hall and nearly fell into the moat for his pains!

Then there were stories of the tunnels. Tunnels built long ago, deep underground, that stretched from the hall to Holy Trinity church in Sutton. Many an hour was spent, armed with shovels and spades digging throughout the grounds in the hope the tunnels would be discovered. When time wasn't spent digging for tunnels, there was endless fun to be had playing in the walled garden where a great storm once brought down the wall. Behind the walled garden lies a secret place. At first glance it looks like a simple spinney where bluebells grow but, on further inspection, it all looks a bit odd. The children always wondered why there were two sloping hollows that were divided by an archway made of bricks that lies under a ridgeway that doesn't seem to go anywhere! The brickwork has begun to crumble and is virtually covered in ivy and to walk under it, it is necessary to stoop. Why the archway was built, no one seems to know and one of the children always felt it such a strange place that it scared her and she didn't like going there. The children were told that in Victorian times a Shakespeare play was performed in the spinney, and the red bricked archway was specially built for the actors to enter and exit. That may be so but why the strange feeling of something malevolent? The red bricked arch certainly looks Victorian and, as Mr Owen said, "The Victorians were very secretive about the things that they got up to."

So did one of the Victorian owners, like John Chadwick, of the hall have a "secret place" created for his own secretive purposes or was this the place where the eighteenth century alchemist dabbled in the black arts all those years ago?

Perhaps a more mundane but still disturbing answer could be that the hollows were used for cruel sports such as cock fighting or badger baiting and, after this gruesome activity had taken place, the memory of it, like a dark cloud that threatens rain, still hangs over the hollows.

Another of the children remembers being told that a bomb was dropped on the spinney during the Second World War but got caught in the trees and didn't go off!

So Hopkins the gardener said! Although no one had experienced any direct supernatural activity in the two hollows, the spinney, "Was always a mystery to us!" declared one of the children in later life.

The Story of Wonkey.

Wonkey was a Chinese Pekinese dog who lived at the hall during the 1950's and was loved by all the children, especially, Jean. One night Wonkey could not be found and the children, armed with torches, searched the grounds for him. They eventually found him huddled and scared in one of the corners of the courtyard. To the children's distress they noticed that blood was pouring from his mouth. He hadn't been attacked by a wild animal but out of terror had bitten through his own tongue. His hind legs were also paralysed and remained so until he died. So what had scared him so much that he would bite through his own tongue?

So what other strange things have taken place at the Hall! Quite often garden furniture would be found in the moat but this was put down to the boisterous activity of the local youth rather than to any secret supernatural hand at work!

The Priest's Hole.

In the oldest part of the hall, after clambering up winding stairs, the visitor comes to a series of low beamed rooms. In the bathroom of the Sirius suite near the power shower and soft, white towels lies another of the hall's secrets. At the back of the room a door can be made out and the children were told that it was a priest's hole, a hiding place for priests on the run from the forces of Queen Elizabeth. There is definitely a space behind the door but it now probably leads to the airing cupboard. Small and cramped it may be but any Jesuit would prefer several days of discomfort rather than face the cruelty and humiliation of public execution. It was the children's grandmother who told them the story and it certainly could be the truth as the family who lived in the hall during Elizabeth's reign certainly was a defender of the Roman Catholic Faith.

When the children's grandmother lived in the house the rambling attics were a favourite place where the children liked to play. Doves would sit on the window ledges, ivy tangled itself around the tower and, below, the fish silently swam in the still moat. However, near the attic rooms it seems not everyone is at peace. Along the long corridor walks the "Lady in White." No one knows who she was or why she walks abroad. However, on certain nights she comes down from the tower and then glides along the landing. During the 1920's one of the maids saw the apparition and so disturbing was the presence that the children's Granny called in the local vicar when she moved into the hall in 1923.

Armed with bell, book and candle, the vicar carried out an exorcism, and, although the Lady in White has not been seen in recent years, guests at the hotel still experience coldness in the old part of the hall where the lady in white used to walk.

The manager of the hall, Mrs Parkes, stood on the spot and said, "This is where the strange feeling occurs." The "Strange feeling" continues into one of the bedrooms where the feeling then stops. Guests who have stayed in the oldest part of the hall, where the Lady in White haunts, have also reported feeling, "A cold shiver" come over them followed by a strange noise. The guests would look to where the noise was coming from only to discover that there was nothing there. It seems our spectre in white was a servant girl as she haunts the Red Landing, which was once the servant quarters. However, another theory is that the lady is the wife of Henry Sacheverrel, who died at the beginning of the seventeenth century. She haunts the Red Landing because the timbers of the ceiling are decorated with the family's Coat of Arms. The Coat of Arms, however, reminds her of the heritage that she has lost. Her husband did not bestow the heritage of New Hall to her children but to his illegitimate son, Valens. Valens was the elder of two illegitimate boys from a lady called, "Mistress Keics."

So whether servant girl or dispossessed lady of the manor, walks abroad in the white nightgown no one is quite sure. Maybe she is New Hall's Lady Macbeth, wandering the landings of the mansion in the desperate search for a cure for her sick soul?

Even today the staff of the hall feel uneasy when walking down the corridor where the Lady in White is supposed to haunt.

There has also been another sighting of a spectre from another time. It was the children's Aunty, who saw him. The apparition only lasted a few moments but it was clear and distinct. It was that of a cavalier and he was seen in the kitchen courtyard. The Aunt only reported that she saw him but never really talked about it all that much. This is probably the spectre of Valens Sacheverell as he was a cavalier and fought for the forces of the King during the English Civil War. It is recorded that in 1645, Valens was charged with, "Compounding for delinquency in deserting his house for enemy quarters." This means he allowed Royalist troops and supporters to live in the house. It is even said that Charles 11 stayed at the Hall when fleeing from England. For his pains, Valens was fined the princely sum of £542, a considerable amount of money in the seventeenth century. Maybe then, Valens made a brief return to his former home to ensure all was well and that England once more was in the safe hands of the monarchy.

Although not supernatural, certainly of great historical interest, is the Diamond writing which can be found scratched on the window frames in the Great Hall. Most of it is written in Latin and was probably written by George Sacheverell, who is also the chief candidate for being Doctor Sacheverell, the alchemist of New Hall. The writings are signed and dated 1689. Quite a few of the quotations have political and religious themes but two seem to refer to affairs of the heart.

October 20th 1689.

QUAE FECISSE IUVAT FACTA REFERRE PUDET which means, What you enjoyed doing you are ashamed to talk about.

Then only nine days later George writes, again in Latin,
QUOD CRIMEN DICIS PRAETER AMARE MEUM, which means, what do you call my crime but loving.

The words, "Ashamed" and "Crime" suggest something illicit and even sinister! Was George involved in an illicit or dubious relationship with one of the women in the hall? Whatever the words mean or refer to, certainly caused him distress and, like that of our Lady in White, it seems his soul was afflicted.

Had he woven a spell from his alchemist's books that had not gone quite accordingly to plan? Several of the Sacheverells were suspected of magical practices and dabbling where they shouldn't.

The Sacheverell family lived in the hall spanning the sixteenth and seventeenth centuries and it seems George is the almost infamous Dr Sacheverrel. His knowledge was deemed, "In advance of his time." Along with several other members of the Sacheverell family, who were suspected of practising magic and other occult sciences, the not so good doctor was known as the, "Alchemist of New Hall." Such was his infamy that a poem was written, not about him but to him, warning him of his dangerous deeds.

The alchemist referred to in the poem is certainly George as he died without issue. The lines of one of the stanzas is as follows:

Sullen Sacheverell, last of thy race,
Of New Hall's fair lands to be master,
Leave magic and alchemy, fly from this place,
Thou art warned of impending disaster.

It is widely believed that George had a secret study somewhere in the hall where he practised his dark arts. No one knew where it was. However, when a passage known as the Screens was taken down when the hall was being renovated a room was discovered. It lay on the side of the Great Hall and like the said room was oak panelled. It well may have been the place the "Warlock of New Hall" cast spells and spoke to the dead! Was it also in this room that George Sacheverrel was visited by a demon and made a pact with the devil? Again, a contemporary poem of his day was written where the alchemist has a conversation with a demon that was summoned up from the depths of hell. Like Mephostophilis in Dr Faustus, the demon warns Sacheverrel of his search for knowledge and prosperity by embracing the occult.

Mephostophilis warns Faustus with the words,

"O Faustus, leave these frivolous demands,
Which strike a terror to my fainting soul."

Act 1. Scene 3.

Likewise, our own Dr Faustus is issued with a warning.

"Vain is thy search, and fruitless thy task,
Some things will always be hidden,
What is to come, thou shalt not ask,
Mark what I say: THOU ART BIDDEN."

Locals say that the ghost of the doctor haunts the grounds of the hall by the mill. A local historian and librarian says there is a grove near the mill where she refuses to go as she feels there is a presence of evil there and offers no rational explanation why she feels like this.

Perhaps at a more mundane level, George may have been a victim of prejudice. He was a Jacobite and Catholic sympathiser, so much that he was under house arrest at New Hall. So instead of being visited by a demon he was in turn, demonised because of his religious and political views! Whatever, he certainly was an intriguing man that has led to a fascination following him down the centuries!

Another incident took place in the house in the winter of 1957. The children's grandmother, who had lived in the house, died. She died at five o'clock in the morning in her bedroom on the first floor. After she passed away, saddened and stunned they came downstairs and sat to recover themselves. They sat there quietly for an hour or two while their father comforted their grieving aunt. In the distance they could hear the sound of a bell tolling. No one remarked on it and carried on sitting in silence, and nothing was said.

Later that day the team of nurses changed shift and the day nurses arrived. They came into the room and they said, "Why is the bell tolling?" The children looked at each other and remarked, "Oh yes, it has been tolling." Then it suddenly dawned on them that the bell could not be tolling, as, although there was an old bell in the ancient tower, there wasn't a rope to ring it with! Also, at this point the day nurses were unaware that their grandmother had died! To this day no one can give a satisfactory explanation as to how the bell tolled that day.

To conclude, with as with the paranormal activities in Sutton Park, New Hall has some strange happenings that can only be heard and not seen. When the Owens lived in the Hall, one quiet night, whilst they were at dinner, a loud crash could be heard coming from an adjacent room. Those at dinner left their places and rushed to where the noise was coming from. They expected a large antique painting to have fallen from the wall or one of the splendid chandeliers, to have crashed to the floor. However, when they entered the room they soon noticed that nothing was out of place and the room was as it was previously.

In the grounds of New Hall, not far from the moat, lies Yew Tree Walk. It is an enchanting avenue of trees that leads to a circle of trees. It is said that in the evening and well after dark, if you wander down through the grounds to the Magic Circle and are lucky enough to be there when the moon and hour is right you will hear voices from another time.

The noises of a carriage with galloping horses can be heard. They gallop with such urgency that one wonders why the whip is cracked so ferociously and why the horses run with such speed.

Maybe it is something to do with our friend, Valens Sacheverrel, the dashing cavalier who was fined so heavily for allowing Royalists to be billeted in the Hall. Or could it have been the sounds of a secret visitor being whisked away to a safe haven in another land? The story goes that there was a visitor that stayed at New Hall. He was a man on the run, a fugitive, hounded by the Government's soldiers. If he was caught he could expect no mercy. The young man that fled New Hall that night was not only a young dashing cavalier, but also the Heir to the throne of England, Prince Charles.

New Hall, ancient moated house.

Corridor, where the ghost of the Lady in White walks abroad.

Declan's Story.

Now, gentle reader, if we were to move a little further up the lane from New Hall, the lane that stills retains its rural curves; there are still stories to be told. Travel with me to one Sunday morning in the year 1966. England had just won the World Cup and a local family were leaving morning mass.

Although it was summer there was still a mist hovering over the fields by the church of the Holy Cross. The church can be found on Signal Hayes Road in Walmley. Declan, the son of Irish parents who had settled in the area, would walk along the woods and fields by Newhall on their way home. His dad would tell tales of how they would catch pheasants back home in Ireland. Then, suddenly out of the mist came a man on a horse. The horse and rider could be made out trotting along the recently ploughed field. What caught Declan's attention was the size of the horse, which he later described as being, "At least eighteen hands high." The man on the horse wore a dark green cloak and on his head was what could be best described as a three cornered hat. The rider held a riding crop in his hand and a young lad led the horse and was walking slowly in front. Declan also noticed that the rider's hair was tied back with what seemed like yellow ribbons.

At first Declan and his Dad thought there was nothing out of the ordinary as Walmley in the 1970's lay virtually in open country on its eastern side. "Perhaps it's the game keeper from the Hall," was Declan's Dad's declaration.

However, what was odd was there was no noise and the horse, rider and boy seemed to gently pass along than physically plod across the field. Father and son walked on. They looked again to where the horse and rider were, only to see them gone, disappeared in the late morning mist. They had only gone a few yards down the road when to their astonishment they noticed the horseman and boy. Except this time the two were on the other side of the road and in another field!

A week or so later Declan's Dad met the game keeper from New

Hall and recounted his strange experience in the hope that he might be able to shed some light on the mystery. The gamekeeper, having heard the tale, retorted in a flat, Warwickshire accent, "No one rides horses round here."

Declan and his father were none the wiser as to who or what they saw that Sunday but Declan's Mother warned them not to speak of it any more.

The Hooded Figure of Fox Hollies.

It seems that Walmley is home to many strange apparitions. In the early Eighties a local man called John Bailey was cycling home from Minworth where he worked. It was a winter's night and there was little or no natural light. He had just turned into Oxleys Lane from Fox Hollies when he saw a figure on the other side of the road. The figure had come from a clump of trees and walked towards John so he put his brakes on, thinking that the stranger was about to ask for directions. John stopped. The figure came closer and closer to him as if gliding towards him. Slightly alarmed, John leant back, as the figure got nearer and to John's amazement walked through him!

John was obviously startled at the time. He looked behind but the figure had gone and, after a few seconds he looked down the lane to see if he could see the figure. There was nothing there. He sat on his bicycle, breathing deeply until he had composed himself and then cycled off home. John described the figure as being, "Strangely dressed." He was hooded, like a monk, and he wore a large key and chain around his waist. He could not distinguish any feet and certainly not his face. John said, "It was just a figure that startled me at the time,"

He had thought, as it was a hooded figure, it was one of the workmen coming back from the fields, as hooded jackets were quite fashionable at the time.

There was no wind that evening and, although dark, it wasn't too dark for him to make out it was a person. John simply thought that it was a person trying to have a conversation with him! John was unable to give any rational explanation for his experience but it was "Perfectly real as he came straight into me. It was a curious phenomenon and I have never forgotten it."

However, he had heard that there were once monks who settled in Langley Heath. There was an article in the local paper that reported strange goings on in the area. There are quite a few sightings around the old stable block of what was once Langley Hall. The stable block and outhouses have now been converted into luxurious apartments.

However, he is not alone in witnessing strange goings on in the area. "Other things have been seen," he said. Driving down the same road one night, a couple of young men suddenly saw a figure walking in front of them at the crossroads. They had to brake suddenly. They shouted out, "Look where you are going. " No sooner had they finished their berating, than the figure disappeared as quickly as it had appeared.

Also, a strange face has been seen peering in one of the windows at Langley Heath.

It is that of a lady wearing an old fashioned dress. She just looks sadly out of the window! A policewoman who moved into one of the apartments in the hall soon put her flat up for sale when she realised that she was sharing with a poltergeist!

The new apartments were once the home to the Pudsey family, a rich and noble family in the parish. Their family vault can be found at Holy Trinity the church on the hill near the centre of the town. William Wilson, an architect and stonemason from Sutton, married the recently widowed, Jane Pudsey. William was both young and handsome but the wealth lay with Jane.

Jane's relatives were appalled at the marriage as she was certainly marrying beneath her social station and class. How could she leave the splendour of Langly Hall to spend the rest of her life with a mere stonemason! Maybe the face at the stable window is a disapproving one as she watches the groom prepare Jane's horse or perhaps angry words are exchanged as Jane mounts her horse and canters off over the cobblestones leaving Langley for ever. The disappointed visage is a sad reminder of her powerlessness to stop Jane as she leaves the moated manor for a new life with William.

The Lady in White.

More recently about a mile away where the supermarket, Asda, now proudly stands a tale of a very strange happening can be told. A young woman, Helen, was driving home one chilly night in September with her boyfriend, Jason, when they noticed a woman walking down the lane that runs at the back of the supermarket. As they got closer to the woman they noticed that she was dressed all in white and that she wore what could be described as a long Victorian petticoat and a bonnet upon her head. They drove past her but curiosity got the better of them and when they reached the traffic island they turned around and headed back towards the woman in white.

It had only taken them about thirty seconds to turn round but their mystery woman had moved at an alarming rate and was now several hundred yards up the lane. When they neared the woman they slowed down. The woman in white also stopped and looked at them. Helen "freaked out" and begged Jason to drive on.

They soon returned to Jason's parents, in a state of shock and Helen was quite disturbed at the sighting. Jason's father left the comfort of his warm house and drove down the lane but there was no woman to be seen. Helen and Jason were unable to explain what they saw that night. However, a friend of Jason's family said that long ago Quakers, or The Society of Friends to give them their proper name, used to live in the area and would often be seen walking in the fields. Historically this can be backed up as the Society of Friends, the proper title for Quakers, built a Meeting House at Wigginshill in Sutton Coldfield. It has been described as a convivial place. As there was only one meeting place in the area, all the Quakers from as far as Wishaw and Coleshill would travel to meet their fellow brethren. Most of them were agricultural workers and on the Sabbath they could be seen crossing the fields on their way to Wigginshill. The Quakers had worked hard and with enthusiasm to build their Meeting House. Numbers declined and the Meeting House closed in the early part of the Nineteenth Century. It no longer stands on the site but the gravestones of the Quakers are still in place.

Jane, another local lady, has also seen the, "Lady in white." Jane lives on a newly built housing estate near the superstore and one autumn night she was restless and found it hard to sleep. She heard footsteps outside the house and got up to investigate. The footsteps were audible and were described by Jane, "As if a child was walking in her mother's shoes." Jane looked out of the window. It was nearly dawn and there, walking through the estate, was an elderly lady dressed all in white. Her dress was ankle length and she wore a shawl over her shoulders. Jane also noticed a white cat walking near the lady in white!

According to Jane there are no elderly people living on the estate and if they were, surely they would not be walking around at 4.30. in the morning, even if Asda is open twenty-four hours a day! So maybe our mysterious lady in white is a Quaker, making her way to the MeetingHouse at Wigginshill for her Sunday service.

Quaker Meetinghouse at Wigginshill, near Walmley.

The Ghost of Manor Hill.

A Mrs Lampitt telephoned one evening with a strange tale to tell. On the West Side of Sutton behind the Cup at Maney, public house lies Manor Hill. There is an old house there where strange goings on have been noted. When Mrs Lampitt was a little girl, (her name is Margaret) she used to go to the old Manor House, as her Mother was the cleaner. She would walk up the sweeping drive past the tennis courts, until she came into view of the grand, huge, old house. There were so many rooms in the rambling old house. Margaret had come into; "Another world" as this house had so many rooms. There was a breakfast room, a scullery, study, snug, and a library. There was even a special room where they kept all the baskets for the garden when the family would collect flowers. Surely it would have tales to tell? However, "Our Maggie" was slightly scared as she helped her Mom clean the rooms. She made sure that she did not stray too far away for she was convinced that she was not alone!

"There was a feeling that there were other people there you could not see!" It was Margaret's job to empty the waste paper bins in the bedrooms. She made sure that she emptied them quickly and always ran up and down the stairs because she always felt that there was someone else with her! Also, if she left doors open, on her return they would be closed.

It was also Margaret's job to polish the intricate, engraved banisters on the stairs. She knew what stairs creaked so she always stepped over them. However, no matter how often she stepped over the creaky steps she could hear the creak seconds afterwards!

Even in the huge garden Margaret felt that she was never on her own.

The Foster family used to live there and they had two dogs. The dogs always slept in the breakfast room. When Margaret entered the breakfast room the dogs would look at her as if they recognised her. However, they then barked soon after, barking at someone who wasn't there.

Margaret's Mom used to relate many tales and stories to her about the strange happenings at Manor Hill. One night Mr and Mrs Foster held a dinner party and lots of guests were invited. Mr Foster left the dinner party to go upstairs. On his way he came across a lady who looked quite lost. Thinking she was one of the guests, he asked her if he could help her and, as he did so, she disappeared into the main bedroom. Mr Foster, naturally, followed her into the room. She then went through the wall into his dressing room and disappeared!

There was another tale; the children of the house had a party. They were teenagers and for their amusement they were playing Postman's Knock and one of them had to leave the room. Whilst waiting outside the room the young man turned round to see the figure of a "Grey Lady". She walked through the dining room door and then through the study door. He became very scared and the dogs started to bark. The other young people left the party and much to the children's astonishment, they saw a figure of a lady on the stairs. She appeared for a brief moment before disappearing.

An article on the subject of Manor Hill appeared in a well-known national magazine. It is also said that that there is a tunnel that leads from the cellars of the house to Sutton Park and was constructed during the time of Cromwell.

It is well known that a Manor House once stood on Manor Hill probably since Norman times. The Norman lords, although keen on pursuits like hunting and feasting, were aware that there were other needs as well as corporal ones. Hence, soon after the manor house was built, a chapel dedicated to Saint Blaize was erected. The Manor House and chapel stood proudly on the hill looking down into the valley. In the valley nestled the growing village, surrounded by plentiful pools of water.

Miss Bracken, a local Victorian historian wrote in 1860 that the site of the original manor house was "Perfectly traceable." The house where Margaret had her experiences as a young child, as did the boys at the party, is almost certainly the site of the original manor house. Steeped in history and folklore it is no wonder then that people from another time make a visit. Like with many old houses it may be a previous owner or lover of the house whose affections for the house are too strong and he/she is unable to leave. In a way it sounds idyllic so maybe the lady that still frequents the "Manor House" does not wish to leave!

For the reader more interested in the macabre it is possible to leave the tale on a more sinister note. Local legend would have it that Maney, the area where the Manor House stood, was a place of ill omen as the Druids practised their religious rites there. It is not for us to judge the good or evil of anyone's religious rites but, If there is evil there, it is a refreshing thought to think that St Blaize, who is the patron saint of wild animals, would be able to chase any demons away!

Moxhull Hall.

A lorry driver driving down the A38 one winter's night was forced to abandon his journey as the snow was falling fast and thick, making driving both difficult and dangerous. He turned off the road and came across Moxhull Hall. The hall is a very charming building whose appearance somewhat deceives. With its lead stained windows and Tudour styled windows that etch into the deep blue of a winter's night it could belong to a far off century. The oak staircase at the entrance of the hall is said to come from Kenilworth Castle.

However, it is an Edwardian building and the old Moxhull Hall stood where the Belfry stands today. In the last years of Victoria's reign the original house was visited by the deadly tuburculosis virus and several children died. The master of the house was a man called Mr Ryland who was distraught as the disease ravaged through the ancient hall. Due to lack of medical knowledge and science one theory was that the virus that was causing the illness was present in the wood-work. Those dreadful symptoms of coughing blood and aching limbs, like a biblical pestilence, had visited the hall.

The house caught fire one night and was burnt to the ground and to this day it seems it was burnt down in mysterious circumstances. To ensure his lineage Mr Ryland built a new Moxhull a mile or so away from the diseased, ravaged site.

Our lorry driver found refuge there that winter's night and was greeted by Mr Bowden, the manager who soon gave him a warm bed for the night. He was not alone, as guests had been unable to leave because of the snow and other drivers caught in the snowdrift had also abandoned their vehicles and sought warmth and comfort at the hall. They could see the hall, and with a certain amount of difficulty, crossed the snow-laden fields and trudged their way to the hall. The famous Crufts Dog Show and a fashion show were taking place at the N.E.C, which is not too far from the hall.

It seemed all of England was huddled under one white wintry blanket. It was like the war, one person remarked. The electricity was down and people gathered around candles, sat in the once Edwardian drawing room and shared stories.

It was like a modern version of "The Canterbury Tales," as narratives and adventures were exchanged late into the night.

As the night deepened, sleep got the better of the Hall's impromptu guests and soon they clambered up the old oak stairs to the cosy rooms that were waiting for them. However, our lorry driver friend awoke during his brief stay and for some reason went downstairs. There by the fireplace in the main hall he saw the spectre of a little girl. She was about eight years old and just stood by the fireplace before disappearing. This was the first sighting of a spectre in the house.

There are other stories connected to the hall. First of all there are the reported sightings of ghosts in room 21 and room 23 which are at the back of the building. People from all over the world who have stayed at the hotel have told stories of their experiences. Some of them have woken up in the morning shivering at what they have seen. A very interesting event took place in the Bridal Suite, which is Room 21. The happily married couple took a photograph of their marital bed, a four -poster.

When the photograph was developed not only was there a picture of the bed but an image, a ghostly image, of a child lying on the bed. The couple were adamant that they hadn't taken any photographs of children or babies on the film, which could have explained the image.

An Italian gentleman used to stay in Room 23. He would come down in the morning and say; "There is a ghost in my room." He went on to say that there was the ghost of a lady in his room. His lady in white would appear at exactly the same time each evening when he was staying there. However, other guests that have stayed in the room have seen the figure of a man standing at the end of the bed.

In room 21 a woman has often been seen. One man after a wedding woke up in a very distressed state. In fact he was described as being, "Beside himself" after experiencing an apparition in Room 21. He said he felt all cold and tingling. He tried to wake his wife up but to no avail and the next morning he vowed never to return.

Quite a lot of people have witnessed activity on the front lawn. The kitchen maids, when arriving in the early morning, have heard children singing on the lawns outside, only to look and find no one there.

One night the lady of the house was staying in the hotel. She woke up during the night and she heard a lady singing and these children laughing. She described it as an old fashioned lullaby.

"I woke up during the night and thought I was dreaming. I went back to sleep again. Three times I heard it and I thought it was coming further down the corridor. It was soothing and the children were laughing. I thought that was nice and never thought anymore about it. I just assumed it was a guest. I thought what patience she had, singing to the children all night.

"I said to the receptionist on my way out if the people had left and she told me that there had been no one up there all night."

However, according to the lady of the house, the voices and the singing sounded perfectly normal and it was as if residents were in the room. The people who lived in the hall before the present owners had heard children singing, as did the chambermaids. However, when a nursery was opened the children's singing stopped. Perhaps the house likes children and wanted them there.

To back this up one need go no further than the restaurant. Inside the restaurant there is a magnificent, oak carved fireplace. It is dated 1878 or 1778. There is a portrait of a young couple carved into the wood but they seem to belong to the Georgian period more than the Victorian or Edwardian period. The style of the costume suggests that the fireplace is older than the house and was brought either from the original Moxhull Hall or from another stately home. What also are interesting are the carvings on the fireplace of children and cherubs. On the adjacent wall there are also carvings of storks, the birds that traditionally bring children.

If we go back slightly in time we may find the answers. A lady called Barbara told Julie, the lady of the house, that before the war, children would be invited during the summer to come to the hall and enjoy the grounds of the house.

They would arrive on the back of farmers' hay carts. They then enjoyed the delights of playing in the summer sunshine. Are these the voices of the children that have been heard by so many guests and workers at Moxhull?

There are also reports of apparitions outside the hall near the old water tower. Two lads one dark night were walking by the tower when they saw a shadowy figure pass by. They did not know what it was but whatever it was they ran and kept running until they reached the sanctuary of Wishaw Village. They banged on the door of a friend, a local man, and begged to be let in and stay the night.

Another happening took place just outside the main entrance of the hotel. A figure seemed to cross what is now the car park. No age, costume could be made out but it certainly was a figure shrouded in light that passed quickly across the empty car park.

Moxhull Hall. Children can be heard playing on the lawn.

Four poster bed where picture of ghostly child was seen!

Holy Trinity Church and High Street.

A young man making his way to the parish church of Holy Trinity one Sunday morning saw a man walking down the hill. There is nothing extraordinary in that, except there was a grey shadow hovering and following the man! The shadow soon became the figure of a woman walking in a mist!

Another tale about the church is that originally it should have been built at Maney Hill. The stones that were to be used to build the church were brought to the site. However, by the next morning the stones had disappeared. Locals said spirits had come and taken the stones to Trinity Hill as it was there the church should be built!

The church hasn't any known ghosts but is unusual in that it is not built from east to west like most churches. Also the vaults in the church seem to be very good in fulfilling the Biblical prophecy, "From dust thou came and to dust thou shalt return."

In 1762 the, "Gentleman's Magazine" of the day gives this description.

"In two of them (Vaults) lately opened corpses have been found to be reduced to mere dust, together with the coffins of wood which enclosed them, the interment of which has been within the memory of man."

The small but verdant churchyard is also the last resting-place of Mary Ashford, who was mysteriously murdered one May morning in 1817.

Near Holy Trinity, on the old High Street, a local gentleman called Mr Wallwork worked at what is now Number One but was originally Number Three before the coach house was knocked down. The premises were the site of a b ank before Mr Wallwork moved in. There are stories of a secret tunnel that leads from the church to the Three Tuns and passes beneath Number Three. In the old coach house stone steps led down into a cellar which is thought to be an entrance to the secret tunnels.

There was a long corridor and at the end a large, strong room door.

It was in the corridor that you could hear children giggling with the, pitter, patter of little footsteps coming and going. Sometimes there were at least two children and sometimes there was only one. The footsteps would soon die away; followed by a giggle which Mr Wallwork was certain was a girl's. There is also a room at the back of the building that overlooks what was once a large garden. It was in this room that the sound of children laughing could be heard and the room would go icy cold when the children's laughter could be heard. As soon as the laughing stopped the room would become warm again. "It was quite eerie," Mr Wallwork said. And although the experience was eerie Mr Wallwork was sure the children were happy and there was no threat or danger, just, "Happy children laughing."

Mostly the voices the laughter would come at night when Mr Wallwork was working alone at night. People who worked in the office also heard the children's voices and felt the coldness. So who are these children whose disembodied voices can still be heard till almost the present day? According to Mr Wallwork, the building was a family home to a local doctor for many years.

Next door, at Vesey House, a retired gentleman used to tell Mr W about ghosts in his part of the building. Mr Wallwork would often come across the elderly gentleman in the garden whilst he was cleaning his Rolls Royce car.

He told Mr Wallwork that there was a connecting door between number 5 and number 7 and that would mysteriously open itself over night. It would be locked at night only for it to found open the next day. Everyone was mystified by it. The opening of the door happened several times.

It also seems that number 5 is home to a tragedy as related by the retired gentleman. It involves a young child and a robin. A family lived in number five during the reign of Queen Victoria and they had a son. One day he went missing. They called the police and searched everywhere but to no avail. The police were called and suspicion fell on a band of travelling folk who had been in the area visiting the town's fayre. The police thought that the travellers had kidnapped the boy and were planning to hold him to ransom. However, there was no proof and they were allowed to continue on their way.

However, some time after, the parents noticed that a robin kept coming and perched itself on the kitchen window sill that over looked the back garden. The robin would then fly down to the bottom of the garden and land on a twig that was sticking up from the earth. He then would fly back to the windowsill and back to the twig again. Curiosity eventually got the better of the father and he went to investigate. When he came to where the robin would land, much to his horror he discovered it was not a twig at all but a finger, a finger of a little hand sticking out of the soil. His child had been murdered and buried there, in the bottom of the family's garden.

Again, suspicion fell on the gypsies but again there was no proof. However, from that day onwards there has always been a robin in that garden and Mr W testified that his garden, that was next to number five, was always visited by robins.

Fox Hill Farm.

Just off the road near old Moor Hall lies the Hungry Horse Tearoom. It has a lovely vista that overlooks the undulating Warwickshire countryside. However, the Hungry Horse, a welcoming watering hole to many a traveller, was a farmhouse a long time ago. Sadly, there is one occupant of the Hungry Horse who believes that time has not moved on.

The spectre is that of an elderly Victorian lady who has been seen sitting by the fireplace in what is now the tearoom and is also prone to move objects about. Sue who works there related the time when her mug of coffee was mysteriously moved by an unseen hand. Sue then discovered the mug several minutes later in the other room.

One day Sue was busily preparing for the day ahead. As she was at her work she felt that some one was looking at her. She turned around and there, framed in the doorway stood the figure of a middle aged Victorian lady. Sue turned back to the sink, waited a few moments and then looked back. Again the lady was still there but vanished after a few seconds.

The sighting where the Victorian lady was seen is very important. Although she was seen in the frame of kitchen door, in Victorian times it would have been the front door of the farmhouse. In the past, Fox Hill farm was well known for its poultry and that the farmer's wife would come to the door as local people called wanting to buy her eggs.

Apparently, she also met a tragic death. A local lady with psychic abilities came to the Hungry Horse for afternoon tea. During her brief stay there she became very upset. She said that she could see a lady in a rocking chair by the fire. Then, to her horror, she saw the old lady engulfed in flames! After her "visitation" and visibly shaken, she said that the old lady had been tragically killed in a fire. The lady also said that the lady was, "Very unhappy" because she did not know she was dead!

She has also been seen standing in the fields. The family who lived in the farmhouse, prior to its conversion, often felt uncomfortable. The children of the house at the time often talked about, "Hearing and seeing things," and their parents would never leave them in the farmhouse alone.

To stay with the theme of children, one of the helpers who works at the tearooms invited her family for a meal. Her four -year old, nephew turned around to his mother and said, "Who is that lady with the children in the corner?" His mother looked around only, obviously, to see the corner empty.

However, it seems there is a more sinister presence at Fox Hill. One autumn afternoon after the skies had gathered and the light had faded into night, Sue was about to experience something quite fearful. The last of the tables had been cleared and the last customer had said farewell. It was the end of a weary day. As the last table was being wiped she looked up and, to her amazement; a hooded figure was peering through the window. The apparition only lasted a few seconds but it struck fear into her. She soon became anxious and wanted to leave immediately.

It is desperately sad, to think that a spirit, a soul, is trapped at the farm. If this is the truth, let us hope and pray that she may be released from her purgatory. As for the hooded figure at the window we can only surmise. Was it something conjured up from, "The heat oppressed brain," or was it something more?

A local man called Trevor remembers that the Cope family lived there. He used to work on their farm during the 1950's. The lady of the farm, Annie Cope, would have been in her seventies and her daughter, Marie, would have been in her fifties. Therefore, Annie Cope would have been born in Victorian times but would not have been a Victorian lady. Trevor said that he had felt a presence when he had been in a tea room and there was, "Talk of a fire." Was then some terrible tragedy that the family experienced, perhaps we shall never know?

Hungry Horse Teas Rooms once Fox Hill Farm.

Victorian Lady at
farmhouse door.

Sutton Court Hotel.

From The Sutton Court Hotel, which lies on the corner of the Lichfield and Sutton Road, comes the tale of a ghost of a different kind. The hotel cannot boast a lady in white or a hooded medieval figure but it can tell of the tale of the ghost with a tail! For the hotel is haunted by the ghost of a dog!

Peter Bennet, the hotel owner, claims that the dog, which haunts the premises, is a victim of a double tragedy. Before the hotel was converted from houses a double tragedy took place during the 1940's. One night a woman was burned to death in a fire and when her husband discovered her body he died of a heart attack. Their dog, in turn, became an "Orphan."

The orphan dog is apparently a King Charles Spaniel and he is seen at least two to three times a year and especially on the eve of Hallowe'en. Mr Bennet also has a King Charles Spaniel called Benjamin. This year he left Benjamin with the night porter, Michael Bott, so that Michael would have some company, and anything else that might put in an appearance.

For as well as the spooky spaniel, apparently, there is another visitor from another time in the hotel but he is not a furry friend. It is said that in one of the rooms, if you look in the mirror, you see a different face looking back at you, smoking a cigarette by all accounts

The Ghost of Sutton Library.

People shuffle in from cold, wet streets, seeking shelter from the rain but also seeking to escape from the fear and uncertainty of war. There, on the screen, Bogart is playing. Cigarette smoke almost clouds the screen. A young lady in her usherette uniform shines a torch to show a late comer to his seat. He is tall and handsome and is quite an attraction to the local girls as he's a GI from the United States, which has just entered the war. This American GI chats up the pretty usherette as she showed him to his seat. He later gets the young lady's name by giving a fellow usherette a "Bribe" in order that he can ask her out for a date. She did go out for that date. She got to like him and later married him! However, there seems to be someone who was at the Empress whose story is not so happy.

The present day Sutton Library is the site of the Empress Cinema. One night when the library was closing the security officer, Vic Brooks, was checking the rooms to make sure everyone had gone home. One Friday evening several years ago, a regular dance group was about to leave. A gentleman, one of the members of the group walking out of the library, turned back to look into the children's library and, quite puzzled, said to Vic.

"Have you got a ghost in the building?

Vic replied that the library had a reputation for being haunted.

The gentleman replied, " I have just seen a ghost of a lady in white sitting in a chair. Don't worry. She's no harm in any way."

Vic was polite but dismissed it with healthy cynicism. Vic then went into the children's library to lock up. As he went into the children's library he felt an "Eerie sensation." His hair stood on end and Vic also noticed that the temperature had fallen dramatically and that it had become very cold. When he went into the teenager section he felt as if "His brain was being magnetised and was being drawn out of his head!" The place went stone cold. A strange and eerie feeling

On his return the next day there was no sensation or feeling in the children's section but, as Vic emphatically stated, "There definitely was

48

a presence of some one in that room."

So who was the mysterious woman in white? Could it have been one of the many customers of the Empress or was it the spirit of the Usherette as so commonly thought? There is no evidence of any air raid or dramatic death at the Empress so maybe the lady likes to sit there and watch her own picture show.

Empress Cinema where the library now stands.

Mary Ashford.

During one mist filled morning during the 1930's, a woman was coming home from a shift at Erdington laundry. Tired from her labours the lady came across a lady, "All in white" with a basket of eggs by the gate at Plantsbrook River on Penns Lane.

The woman who saw the apparition was Pat Sinsheimer's Mother who lived at Bracebridge. She knew straight away that it was Mary Ashford. "She just knew, she just knew" was Pat's reply when asked how her Mother knew it was Mary Ashford.

It is certain that Mary had a basket on the night she died but no one can be sure whether it would be full of eggs or vegetables. But, as Pat pointed out, it was not just her mother who saw Mary but others as well and maybe they saw Mary at different times and stages of her life. After all, she would have walked up and down Penns Lane many, many times.

In the 1980's a milkman, making his daily delivery in a leafy suburb of modern Birmingham, stopped suddenly, as he could hardly believe what he saw. Coming out of the morning mist was a young woman, dressed in a long dress and bonnet, hurrying along the road. She then vanished. The milkman was confused and perplexed. Sometime after, near the same spot, a British Telecom engineer received an electric shock whilst digging in the street. Fortunately, he was more shaken than injured. Were these incidents in any way related to Mary and that heinous crime that took place almost two hundred years ago?

One fine English May morning near where the turnpike road separated the hamlet of Erdington from the boundaries of the parish of Sutton Coldfield, a young labourer called George Jackson was walking across the dew covered fields. As on so many mornings before, he had walked from his humble house in Curson Street, Birmingham, to work at Penn's Mill. The sun shone and the sky was clear blue. George was probably thinking of the day's work that lay ahead of him. George Jackson, like nearly all of us, would have lived out his life, lived and died, on the stage of this world and like a leaf in a November wind would have been blown away into the winter of obscurity. However, George made a discovery that morning, a discovery that would not only shock him but horrify the local community and spring open a chain of events that would eventually send shock waves through the English legal system, confound historians, policemen, sleuths and writers for nearly 200 years. It is a mystery yet to be solved. What was it then that George Jackson discovered that May morning?

As he crossed over the fields he saw, what he described as a "lake of blood" in the grass. He followed the trail of bloodstains and noticed footprints, footprints, it seemed, of a man chasing a woman. The woman's footprints stopped abruptly but the man's continued, sunken further into the soil as if by weight, as if a body was being carried. The footprints stopped at the top of a marl pit. There, Jackson saw a bundle of clothes, a bonnet and, neatly placed next to these, a pair of lady's working boots.

Jackson feared the worst and ran to his place of work and shortly returned with help. The pit was dragged with a heel rake and, on the third attempt; a body of a young woman came to the surface. Her name was Mary Ashford and she had, it seems, been brutally raped and thrown in the marl pit to drown. A local farmer and brick layer called Abraham Thornton was promptly arrested and charged with murder. The evidence against him was quite strong.

He was the last man to be seen with Mary after the dance at the Tyburn House. He lied about walking her home. He had Mary's blood on his shirt. He even admitted having sex with her!

He appeared in court in August 1817 at Warwick Assizes charged with the brutal rape and murder of Mary Ashford. After several hours the jury were asked to make a decision. It took them twelve minutes to return a verdict. Abraham Thornton was found not guilty.

Quite simply, Abraham had an alibi; Mary had been seen alone after she parted company from Abraham at around 4.00 am. She died shortly after, but between 4.30 and 5.00 a.m. Thornton was seen three miles away by eight different people. The village, however, cried out for revenge. "Blood will have blood!" was the people's motto. Could Abraham have killed Mary and still be in time to be seen by a host of witnesses, therefore creating an alibi? Was there a conspiracy amongst the witnesses for some unknown reason?

The anger and frustration of the villagers was soon channelled into an ingenious and well thought out plan. Astute lawyers, employed by the Ashford family and supporters, discovered an ancient law whereby an acquitted person could be tried again for the same crime, a facet of law that is now totally alien to our time and culture.

One chilly September evening in 1817, constables of the Crown entered the Thornton farm in Shard End, Castle Bromwich and, as Abraham sat by the hearth, promptly re-arrested him and took him to London where he was to stand trial at the Old Bailey.

The Abraham and Mary case had spread like wild fire to nearly every corner of England. His infamy led to the London mob besieging the courthouse on the day of his trial. The outcome? He was acquitted for the second time. His acquittal came when he was asked if he was guilty or not guilty of the rape and murder of Mary Ashford. A silence fell on the court as he replied, "Not guilty and I am prepared to defend myself with my body."

At this point he produced and threw down a gauntlet, issuing the Norman Law of "trial by battel". The court was thrown into immediate confusion. Thornton's lawyers had been clever, outwitting those of the Ashford family's. They had discovered an unknown law from medieval England, but a law that was still on the statute books. Quite simply it meant he was offering a challenge to his accuser, Mary Ashford's teenage brother, William. If accepted, it meant William would have to fight Thornton, in a roped off field, until one cried, "Yield". If William lost, it meant he had wrongly accused the prisoner and would pay with a lengthy prison sentence: if not, Thornton would be found guilty and pays the ultimate price. That is, if none of them had been beaten to death by the heavy cudgels! It was obvious the burly 25-year-old Thornton would be more than a match for the young William. Lawyers prevaricated, argued and fought. Eventually, a decision was made, the challenge was not taken up and Thornton walked free!

The story, however, does not end happily for Abraham. Indeed, he returned home to Castle Bromwich but was hounded out of the country. He travelled to Liverpool and eventually was allowed to sail on the, "SS Shamrock" bound for New York, never to return to these shores again. Whether he was innocent or guilty we will never know. Was Abraham a victim of mass popular hysteria or was he the "one that got away"? It will always remain a mystery.

Mary was buried at Holy Trinity Churchyard. The Reverend Luke Booker, vicar of Dudley paid for an inscription to be placed upon Mary's tomb. It reads as follows:

As a warning to female virtue
And a humble monument to female Chastity,
This stone marks the grave of Mary Ashford
Who, in the twentieth year of her age,
Having incautiously repaired to a place of amusement
Without proper protection
Was brutally violated and murdered
On 27th May 1817.

However, local legend and folklore combine to say that for several years after Mary's death, her ghost appeared on Penn's Lane looking for justice. It is reputed that she spoke to locals about her tragic plight. The locals wrote down what she said which later became songs known as the "Birmingham Ballads".

However, it seems that the valiant efforts of the local folk musicians may have not been enough.

A theatre group who produced a play about the case experienced all sorts of "weird happenings". When performing at Erdington library the technician noticed that the lights were on full. Nothing unusual in that, except at the time he testified that they weren't plugged in! At the same time the play was being performed, the British Telecom engineer, as mentioned at the beginning of this tale, was nearly electrocuted whilst working on cables in Berwood Road, the site of the pit which Mary was flung. Members of the theatre group also placed flowers on Mary's grave and, despite a severe November frost, they appeared fresh the following week. At the cast party after one of the performances not only did a door that was firmly shut fly open; the lights fused seconds afterwards.

Are all these happenings mere coincidence, the imagination of a nervous cast? Or was it Mary's soul endeavouring to seek justice and finally unravel the mystery once and for all? Let us look again at the inscription on Mary's tomb. After Booker states the cold facts as a warning, "To female Virtue" echoes another, more chilling warning.

Lovely and chaste as the primrose pale
Rifled of Virgin Sweetness by the gale,
Mary! The wretch, who thee remorseless slew,
Avenging wrath, which sleeps not, will pursue
For though the deed of blood be veiled in night,
Will not the judge of all the earth do right?
Fair blighted Flower! The Muse that weeps thy oom
Rears over thy murdered form,
This warning tomb.

Does Mary then, otherwise known as the Lady in White still walk Penns Lane in search of, "Avenging wrath, which sleeps not." Perhaps we shall never know!

Penns Lane where Mary was seen in 1930's.

Mary Ashford's gravestone, Holy Trinity Churchyard.

Mary Ashford looking across fields.

The Lad in The Lane.

The lane still winds its way down into the valley and sweeps along through the fields, until it meets the village, which is marked by the stone cross at the crossroads. Early morning mist hangs over the fields. The only sound that can be heard is the repeated echo of shoes walking along the lane. A smile spreads across a young man's face as he thinks of the revelries he left only an hour or so before. Although day has broken and the early morning sun is slowly waking as it stretches its warm fingers across the furrowed fields, the young man feels somewhat uneasy. He stops and looks around but there is no one there but himself in the lane. He walks on. He gives a glance across his shoulder but there is no one there. He turns to walk on but is frozen by fear. There, before him, is the figure of a boy walking towards him. His clothes looked ragged and out of sorts. The figure walks towards him, and to his horror, the young man realises that the figure has no head!

Although, the young man was alarmed, if not distressed, he need not be too worried for he was not the first person to see the headless body of a boy that was brutally murdered over two centuries ago. Others have claimed to see the hapless boy wandering down Wylde Green Lane. Others have said that, on certain days, at certain times, a skull will appear drifting down the lane much to the amazement, if not fear, of those that witness such an apparition.

Our story, however, gentle reader, does not begin in a meandering English country lane but outside a bawdy public house in Erdington, known as the Tyburn!

The poor boy has been seen there, too, dressed in ragged clothes and calmly sitting on a bench outside the Tyburn. The Tyburn, once in the Parish of Curdworth, was a well-known Coaching House. It lay on the London and Chester Road and was the main artery of transport for the body of England. Many travellers going to or back from London or Ireland would stop off at the Tyburn.

On 4th December 1745 Bonnie Prince Charlie, otherwise known as the "Young Pretender", had reached Derby. The idea of a Scottish army of Highlanders making their way to London to put Charles on the throne struck fear in the heart of nearly every English man and woman. Charles's arrival at Derby was known as, "Black Friday" Rumours ran riot. Some said that the King, George 11, had fled London and that a ship was waiting for him, ready to set sail from the coast. Others insisted that the Scots were as close as Lichfield. The Rector of Holy Trinity, fearing not so much for his life but for the family silver, put it all in a waterproof box and hid it in the fishpond in the rectory garden!

In response to the "invasion" the Duke of Cumberland's army was ordered to march North to meet the rebellious Jacobite army of Bonny Prince Charles. They took a rest from their pursuit and stayed a night in Castle Bromwich at the "Bradford Arms." Apparently much revelry took place and the riotous night ended the next morning with many sore heads!

The colonel of the company was nursing probably the sorest of heads, as he set off the following morning with his men. Due to his enormous hangover he was irritable. Not only that, he became angry when he realised that he had left his sword back at the pub in Castle Bromwich. However, when he came to Bassets Pole a few miles form Castle Bromwich he decided to turn back.

It was on his return, when at the Tyburn, he came across the unfortunate boy. What star the poor boy was born under no one will ever know but it was a tragic day he met with the Colonel from Cumberland's army! The story goes that the irritable officer got lost and asked the boy for directions. The boy had no roof to his mouth and could not speak. The offish man, interpreting the boy's reluctance to speak as an act of treason had the boy arrested. He was charged as being a spy and the colonel gave the order for him to be executed.

This was the price to be paid for apparent disloyalty and treachery. His head was hacked off and paraded on a pikestaff to New Shipton, which is better known these days as Walmley village. His body was dumped in a ditch along the lane, which is now Eachelhurst Road that borders Pype Hayes Park. When the soldiers arrived at New Shipton, to show their disdain they tossed the head into a large oak tree.

Maybe out of fear, we shall never know, but no one in New Shipton or the Tyburn was prepared to retrieve the body and head and give the boy a decent burial and his remains were left for the birds and beasts.

Incredibly, however, in 1823, the body and head of the boy were discovered within a week of each other although a distance of a mile had separated them for seventy-eight years! Is this the lad, then, seen drifting across Wylde Green Road? That poor, innocent boy that was so wrongfully murdered over two centuries ago?

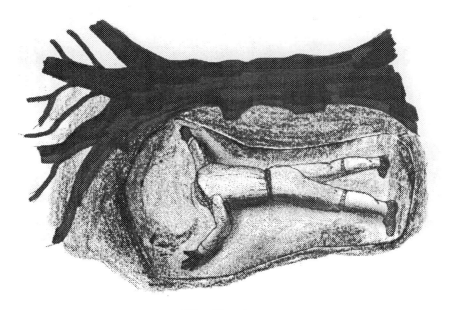

Headless boy.

Stand and Deliver.The story of the highwayman.

The night was fresh and the moon was bright. For most people the day's work had been done. However, for others the day's work was about to begin. The lonely, deserted London to Chester Road was their haunt, their work dangerous but highly rewarding. If successful they could become rich men and live life like a fat squire. However, if they were caught they would end their lives of theft ignominiously on the gallows.

The road is quiet this night but the Highwayman is patient. He's name is Tom and he is a local man. His patience is rewarded as the rattling of a stagecoach can be heard coming towards him. The driver cracks his whip to make the horses go faster as he, along with the couple from London inside, are anxious to pass the dangerous and notorious Coldfield. They are all aware of the nearby "Den", the secret haunt of highwaymen, who could strike at anytime, night or day!

The lamp of the carriage can be made out as the carriage speeds through the night. Suddenly, from the darkness gallops a horse with a rider dressed in black. A mask covers his eyes and a neckerchief his mouth. Then there is a flash and crack as the pistol goes off. The horseman dressed in black shouts, "Stand and Deliver" which echoes through the night air. He then paces around to the window of the carriage where his prize awaits. He spies immediately gold cuff links, a silver pocket watch and the attractive necklace around the lady's neck. He smiles at the lady as he pockets her jewels. However, he is more than a common thief. To soothe the lady and gentleman's nerves he escorts the stagecoach to the border of Sutton Town so that no other Highwayman might put the fear of God into them! Tom did this to all his "Clients" and was known as the Gentleman's Highwayman!

This may seem like a scene from "The Wicked Lady" or "Dick Turpin's last ride" but similar incidents did take place in Sutton Coldfield and it is said that the ghost of the Highwayman still stalks the Chester road looking for more prizes!

Stories abound that the legendary Dick Turpin rode and so did his good friend, Tom King. There was a Tom King who was a Highwayman who came from Stonnal but he wasn't the infamous Tom King who along with Turpin harassed the travellers of Hounslow Heath! It is true to say that cut throats and thieves abounded on and around the Coldfield. It was so dangerous that bowmen in previous centuries could be hired to escort frightened travellers across the common land to safety! In nearby Erdington it is said that both Dick Turpin and Tom King visited the Green Man pub, better known as The Lad in the Lane.

Whatever thoughts we may have of dashing handsome Highwayman living life like an eighteenth century Robin Hood the grim reality can be found not too far from the present site of Oscott College. For it was near the college a man was hanged in 1729 for the murder of a London silk merchant. Some years later a notorious highwayman called Sansbury was arrested along with his fellow robber and they, too, ended their lives at the end of the hangman's rope. These notorious men were not apprehended whilst robbing the London Stagecoach but were discovered drunk in a cornfield.

Eight years later a citizen of Birmingham called Henry Hunt was robbed on the Chester Road. Henry watched in dismay as the assailants took his precious watch and silver. He pleaded for some coins to be returned. The highwaymen agreed but their benevolence was short lived as moments later Henry saw the two rascals rob another unfortunate traveller only yards down the road!

There was a novel published at the end of the eighteenth century entitled, "Spiritual Quixote. " In the book, Lichfield's answer to Don Quixote and Pancho set off for a series of adventures. They soon become lost when they reach the outskirts of Sutton and in the gloominess of the night they see what they think is a signpost. They approach the post only to discover that it is a gibbet with the hanged body of a highwayman swinging in the wind!

So the idea of a highwayman being seen is not based on idle myth or fabrication. It seems there are a few contenders for our, "Knight of the Road." Could it be the notorious Sansbury and his companion? The murderer of the London silk merchant?

Romance would have it that maybe it was Dick Turpin and Tom King who robbed Henry Hunt that day and their ghosts can still be seen as they ride off along the windswept Chester Road, back to the den, laughing wildly, their saddle bags full of booty. To re-enact this adventure would be better than their last moment, that last drop from the gallows.

The Gate Public House.

Karl Bramwell lived with his family at the Gate Public House, which lies at the bottom of the hill by Sutton Town centre. He was alone in the pub one night and after being in bed for sometime he woke up. He felt pressure on the bed as if some one was on sitting it. At first he thought that it must be one of the cats. Then much to his surprise he saw a shadowy figure move off the bed and felt the mattress rise and the bed was at it was before. Although Karl felt slightly confused he certainly wasn't scared. The experience never happened again but previous landlords had experienced strange goings on mainly upstairs in the living quarters. They heard noises and felt as if there were people in rooms when the rooms were empty. One manger did not like being left alone upstairs, as he felt, "uneasy." Karl also said that one of the cats refused to go into a certain room. His partner, Christine also remembers a night when strange goings on occurred at The Gate.

One night after the pub had been shut, Karl, Christine and the bar staff settled down for a quiet drink in the Lounge. They were all enjoying their drink when Christine suddenly said; "I have just seen some one. There's some one in the bar!"

What Christine had witnessed was a figure that she described as, "Tall, dark, solid and probably male". Just as Christine had shouted out, everyone heard the old heavy internal door that linked the bar with the off licence creak loudly as it opened. It then slammed shut. The door was heavy and it was well known that it creaked loudly when opened. Karl immediately went into the passageway that led to the bar. There was no one there. He then walked into the bar. Again it was deserted. Christine had locked the front and side doors that led to the street at closing time and they were still locked. The wind could not have blown the internal door open, as it was too large and heavy. Christine said her experience was indeed chilling and the hairs on everyone's neck did stand up but they weren't really frightened and were sure that whoever or whatever it was, it was a "Friendly ghost."

Karl later said that BBC Radio had visited the pub and spent the night there on a ghost hunt. They set up the appropriate instruments needed to detect spectres but apparently the stranger who slammed the door did not appear! Customers have also reported seeing a figure walk across the bar from one corner to the fireplace.

On the historical side, the pub is a combination of two buildings. The bar is the much older part and the lounge the newer part. Before it was a pub the building was once a garage and perhaps more interestingly, a Toll Gate, hence the name, The Gate. It is also worth noting that Christine experienced the ghost in the old part of the building. It is also said that, like with the nearby Three Tuns, the cellars underneath are part of a complex of tunnels. One of the tunnels leads to the Three Tuns and the other to Holy Trinity, the parish church. There is also the story that they were used as priest's holes during the Roman Catholic persecution of the sixteenth century.

The idea of priests on the run from Elizabeth's soldiers sounds quite exciting. Young men, many who became martyrs, would scamper down holes into damp and dark tunnels. These tunnels would lead to the vaults of the church where they would seek refuge, breathless, with palpitating hearts. In the gloom they would hide, sometimes for days until it was safe to surface and continue their journey again.

Dashing and daring as it might be, imagining priests on the run it would seem that the "Stranger in the bar" is simply a local looking for a pint!

Afore Ye go!

Before you leave the comfort of the fireplace and clamber into bed I would like to leave you, gentle reader, with some supernatural snippets of Sutton.

In the late 1980's the manager of an office in the town centre returned after lunch to find two worried colleagues. He was told that an electric typewriter had started typing on its own. The following words were written,

"The head and in frontal attack on an English writer that the character of this point is there."

At first glance it would seem nothing but gibberish but maybe on closer inspection it could be interpreted as a chilling warning! Could it not be translated as?

"An English writer will be attacked, struck on his head and this is the point of this message."

In nearby Barr Beacon it is reported that bands of local Druids can be seen carrying out their religious rites in an ancient sacred oak grove. It was from the beacon they could study the stars and pray for the spirits of their fellow man and woman who crossed over to the other world.

I received a phone call from a lady who used to live near Rosemary Road in Four Oaks. She told me the tale of the, "Headless horseman" that had been seen in the area. Again, the lady could be said to be a victim of idle chatter, however, it was soon after the phone conversation that this story came to light.

A young man called John Bickley was out riding in the Hill Hook area one summer's day when a sudden storm came upon him. He was struck by lightning and he was killed, along with his horse. It was the first of August 1797. His family, who were local farmers at Hill Hook, had an inscription for their son. It reads:

HERE
On the first of August 1797
JOHN BICKLEY
And the horse which he rode
Were struck dead by lightning

Happily he was an Amiable
YOUTH.

Be Ye also ready.

Matt: 22:44.

Is it possible that the, "Headless horseman" is really the momentary flashback to the tragic incident of John Bickley being struck by lightning that fateful August day?

In nearby Mere Green, in a block of flats there is a figure of a hanging man. Apparently it appears when a certain pane of glass breaks and when the glass is replaced the image of the hanged man can be seen. It reappears in the new pane of glass!

The Post Office, the sorting office in Sutton is supposed to be haunted by a Grey Lady! There is also the ghost of the Grey Lady who haunts Park House in the park. Originally, the house was called Brown's Mill in the eighteenth century. A young woman who lived in the house fell in love with a local man. For some reason or another her family would not allow her to develop their romance.

Undeterred, they continued they relationship in secret. He would leave notes expressing his love for the girl at the mill's oak door. She would creep out of her room during the middle of the night to collect the illicit notes.

The story though does not have a happy ending as the parents discovered the notes and made sure no more were sent. She died of a broken heart. However, she returns ever Hallowe'en looking for her love letters that no longer come.

Another mystery concerns a Jewish woman, who was pedlar selling jewellery in the Midlands. One blustery November evening she set out from the "Bell and Cuckoo" (now the site of the Yenton Pub,

Erdington.). Her intention was to cross the Coldfield to Stonnal but she never arrived. She was supposed to have stayed at one of the two inns at Stonnal but for some reason she never reached there.

She was eventually missed and enquires were made. Even a reward was offered but to no avail. Many years later when the incident became nothing more than a story a new Landlord and Landlady moved into the inn. For some reason business did not go well and word soon got round the village that it was haunted.

One autumn evening, a Harvest Festival was taking place in the inn. The locals were enjoying the fruits of their labours with music and dancing when suddenly an ungodly shriek was heard. The music and dancing immediately stopped and everyone looked towards the fireplace. There stood a woman. Her clothes glowed, like the hands of a luminous clock in the dark. Her face looked so sad. She looked at the revellers for a few moments and then disappeared.

After such a startling apparition the revellers thought it only proper to go home and end all festivities. The new Landlady and Landlord soon left and the house was abandoned. The house soon fell into decay and had to be demolished. Whilst the house was being demolished the workmen came across the skeleton of a woman. Everyone agreed that it was probably the remains of the Jewish lady who had disappeared so long ago. She was buried in the churchyard and all sightings of the ghost ceased.

List of ILLUSTRATIONS AND PHOTOGRAPHS

Illustrations.

Roman Centurion.
Hooves in Park.
Lad in lane.
Mary Ashford.
Woman at Fox Hill farm.
Cavalier

Photographs.

Cover photograph, yet to be decided.
Deserted building by Rowton's well.
Blasted heath where ghostly rider rides by.
New Hall Mill. (Two)
New Hall Hotel. Exterior.
New Hall Hotel. Interior.
Moxhull Hall. Exterior.
Moxhull Hall. Interior.
Three Tuns Hotel.
Hungry Horse.
Mary Ashford. Penns Lane.

Bracebridge Cottage.
Empress Cinema.
Mary Ashford gravestoneand Pens Lane.
Wiggins Hill.

June 5th 2000.   Last revised.

Other works by Patrick Hayes

Short stories.

Ghost Stories of Erdington (1996) published by Brewin Books. A mainly factual yet chilling account of strange goings on in the suburb of Erdington, Birmingham.

Theatre.

Patrick's first play was written during his teacher's training course. Entitled **YOU KNOW WHAT HAPPENED, (1983)** it dealt with the true incident of teenage suicide. It played in London before coming to the Midlands where it won an award for the best original script in a Birmingham theatre festival.

A move back to Birmingham proved productive with the award winning **BUCKETS OF SUNSHINE. (1984).** A mixture of 1940's nostalgia and the horror of the first nuclear holocaust, is the theme for this tragic story. Seen through the eyes of one that was there, the Enola Gay's Catholic chaplain, Father George Zabelka, the play was described as, **"Gripping,"** by the Birmingham Evening Mail. It went on to scoop best play, best actor and best actress awards at the Birmingham F.A.M.E. festival.

BUCKETS OF SUNSHINE was followed by **ANGIE, (1985),** which was written specially for the Sutton College Youth Theatre and gave a harrowing insight into the world of drug abuse.

THE HOUSE THAT JACK BUILT (1987) was the next written piece, a comprehensive examination of the plight of homelessness. The story revolves round five young homeless Brummies who are thrown in the same abject arena as Jack Duggan, a down and out but one time famous Gaelic football star. Due to its popularity it was revived on several occasions and played to full houses at venues throughout Birmingham.

BREAK THE SPELL, (1987-9) was to prove Patrick's most ambitious project. A true story, it re-told the events of the chilling and disturbing Erdington murder mystery of Mary Ashford. Described as, **"Frightening and fascinating,"** by the Birmingham Evening Mail it was performed at the M.A.C. and Coventry Belgrade Studio as well as a plethora of community venues. The story was also subject of Central T.V.'s **CRIMESTALKER,** being narrated by John Stalker.

WHISPER IN THE WINGS. (1989.) As a member of a team of four Patrick wrote a section for the Birmingham Youth Show: A romance in wartime England which was performed at the Birmingham Rep.

LIPSTICK ON THE CHALICE, (1993) was written in support of female emancipation for the Anglican priesthood and was warmly received by aspiring women priests!

TED AND JASS (1994) was part of the Birmingham Readers and Writers Festival. The story revolving around a young Irish Brummie teacher who falls in love with an Asian lawyer. It had a rehearsed reading at the Library Theatre Birmingham.

Film and Television.

Patrick has also written several television and film scripts including **NOT JUST PRETTY FACES, (1989)** a comedy about the obsessive world of "The Pub Quiz."

THE SHUTDOWN (1992) humorously and tragically looks at the decline of a well-known Birmingham tyre factory. Set in the seventies it predicts the doom of closure and looks at the plight of those that choose to fight back.

FACTORY FLOORS AND LOCKER DOORS (1992), is a short

twelve minute film which tackles the thorny issue of pornography. A teenage sister and older brother are the voices in this short but provocative film and was part of the, **STORY SO FAR FILM FESTIVAL, BIRMINGHAM in 1995.**

NOT JUST PRETTY FACES was revived as a stage play for **THE NEW BIRMINGHAM THEATRE** in 1996 and was described in **THE STAGE** as

".... With a first performance of this breezy and robust comedy New Birmingham Theatre serves up the fresh cooked ham, keeping the pace fast and adding some enjoyable comic business."

ONE MORNING IN MAY is the screenplay of the Mary Ashford murder mystery story. It looks at the bizarre and disturbing co-incidences of the murder of Mary Ashford that took place in 1817 and of Barbara Forrest in 1974. Both murders to this day are unsolved.

HARRIET. Based on the Edwardian Suicide Victim in Ghost Stories of Erdington, Harriet tells the story of both romance and intrigue. Since its premiere it has won an award at the Manchester Film Festival of Fantasy and Horror and was available for viewing at the Berlin Film Festival.

Works in progress.

Patrick is currently writing a stage play entitled, **UNDER THE GREENWOOD,** which is a protest play about the controversial Birmingham North Relief Road and a book of 1940's reminisces entitled, **WE'LL MEET AGAIN.**

For further information please contact Patrick on 0121 373 5665 or 0976 825549.